# OUR ABE LINCOLN

## An Old Tune with New Lyrics

# Our Abe Lincoln

Adapted by Jim Aylesworth

Traditional folk song
"The Old Grey Mare"

Our Abe Lin-coln came out of the wil-der-ness,

Out of the wil-der-ness, Out of the wil-der-ness.

Our Abe Lin-coln came out of the wil-der-ness

Man-y proud years a-go.

MAN - Y PROUD YEARS_____ A - GO,

MAN - Y PROUD YEARS_____ A - GO.

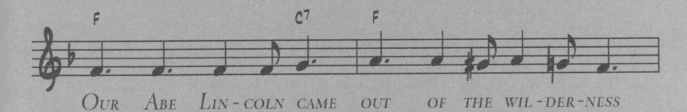

OUR ABE LIN - COLN CAME OUT OF THE WIL - DER - NESS

MAN - Y PROUD YEARS A - GO.

# OUR ABE LINCOLN

An Old Tune with New Lyrics

Adapted by JIM AYLESWORTH
Illustrated by BARBARA McCLINTOCK

SCHOLASTIC INC.
NEW YORK  TORONTO  LONDON  AUCKLAND
SYDNEY  MEXICO CITY  NEW DELHI  HONG KONG

ISBN: 978-0-545-23392-7

12 11 10 9 8 7 6 5 4 3 2 1                    10 11 12 13 14 15/0

Printed in the U.S.A.                    40

First Scholastic paperback printing, January 2010

The display type was designed and created by Kevin Pyle.
The text was set in P22 Parish Roman.
The art was created using pen and ink on watercolor paper.
Music typesetting by Randa Kirschbaum
Book design by Elizabeth B. Parisi

Special thanks to William Furry, Executive Director of the Illinois State Historical Society,
for his consultation on the text and artwork.

Babe Abe Lincoln was born in the wilderness

Born in the wilderness

Born in the wilderness


Babe Abe Lincoln was born in the wilderness

Many long years ago.

Boy Abe Lincoln lived rough with his family

Rough with his family

Rough with his family


Boy Abe Lincoln lived rough with his family

Many cold snows ago.

Smart Abe Lincoln read late by the firelight

Late by the firelight

Late by the firelight

Smart Abe Lincoln read late by the firelight

Many dark nights ago.

Strong Abe Lincoln fell oaks with a mighty axe
Oaks with a mighty axe
Oaks with a mighty axe

Strong Abe Lincoln fell oaks with a mighty axe
Many split rails ago.

True Abe Lincoln was praised for his honesty
Praised for his honesty
Praised for his honesty

True Abe Lincoln was praised for his honesty
Many good deeds ago.

Tall Abe Lincoln made friends there in Illinois

Friends there in Illinois

Friends there in Illinois

Tall Abe Lincoln made friends there in Illinois

Many glad times ago.

Friend Abe Lincoln got sent off to Washington
Sent off to Washington
Sent off to Washington

Friend Abe Lincoln got sent off to Washington
Many campaigns ago.

Kind Abe Lincoln then led as the president

Led as the president

Led as the president


Kind Abe Lincoln then led as the president

Many cruel days ago.

Wise Abe Lincoln said, "NO MORE!" to slavery

"NO MORE!" to slavery

"NO MORE!" to slavery

Wise Abe Lincoln said, "NO MORE!" to slavery

Many brave days ago.

Sad Abe Lincoln spoke grand words at Gettysburg

Grand words at Gettysburg

Grand words at Gettysburg


Sad Abe Lincoln spoke grand words at Gettysburg

Many lost souls ago.

Great Abe Lincoln died hard for the noble deeds

Hard for the noble deeds

Hard for the noble deeds

Great Abe Lincoln died hard for the noble deeds
Many sad tears ago.

Our Abe Lincoln came out of the wilderness

Out of the wilderness

Out of the wilderness

Our Abe Lincoln came out of the wilderness

Many proud years ago.

Many proud years ago
Many proud years ago

Our Abe Lincoln came out of the wilderness
Many proud years ago.

# Author's Note

"Old Abe Lincoln Came Out of the Wilderness" was a popular song during Abraham Lincoln's campaigns for the Presidency and was sung to the tune of "The Old Grey Mare." I have adapted the song into a biography of this famous American.

BABE ABE LINCOLN: Abraham Lincoln was born on February 12, 1809, in a rude log cabin near present-day Hodgenville, Kentucky.

BOY ABE LINCOLN: In 1816, the family moved across the Ohio River to Little Pigeon Creek in Indiana. Sadly, they arrived too late in the season to build a better shelter and had to spend the winter in a very rough half-faced camp.

SMART ABE LINCOLN: With very little schooling available to him, young Abraham Lincoln more or less taught himself how to read and write—sometimes walking miles just to borrow a book.

STRONG ABE LINCOLN: There in Indiana and later when they moved to Illinois, Abe was often hired by neighbors to do the backbreaking labor of splitting rails that were used to make fencing in those days.

TRUE ABE LINCOLN: Once while working as a store clerk in New Salem, Illinois, Abraham Lincoln discovered that he had not given a woman the correct change. That evening, Abraham walked to the woman's home and returned her money. This honest deed and hundreds of others like it earned Abraham his well-deserved reputation for honesty.

TALL ABE LINCOLN: Although tall, awkward, and far from handsome, Abraham Lincoln was well liked for his quick wit and sense of humor. One evening at a dance, he met his future wife, Mary Todd.

FRIEND ABE LINCOLN: Abraham Lincoln was elected President of the United States—November 6, 1860.

KIND ABE LINCOLN: As president, Abraham Lincoln led as our splintered nation suffered through the cruel years of the Civil War—1861 to 1865.

WISE ABE LINCOLN: Abraham Lincoln issued and signed the Emancipation Proclamation, which eventually led to the end of the practice of slavery in the United States—September 22, 1862.

SAD ABE LINCOLN: At the dedication of a war cemetery in Gettysburg, Pennsylvania, a grieving Abraham Lincoln spoke some of the most famous and oft-quoted words in our history, the Gettysburg Address—November 19, 1863.

GREAT ABE LINCOLN: While watching a play in Washington, D.C., Abraham Lincoln was assassinated—April 14, 1865.

OUR ABE LINCOLN: February 12, 2009 commemorates the bicentennial of Abraham Lincoln's birth in that tiny cold cabin in the wilderness of Kentucky—his 200th birthday!

# Our Abe Lincoln

Adapted by Jim Aylesworth

Traditional folk song
"The Old Grey Mare"

Our Abe Lin-coln came out of the wil-der-ness,

Out of the wil-der-ness, Out of the wil-der-ness.

Our Abe Lin-coln came out of the wil-der-ness

Man - y proud years a - go.

MAN - Y PROUD YEARS\_\_\_\_ A - GO,

MAN - Y PROUD YEARS\_\_\_\_ A - GO.

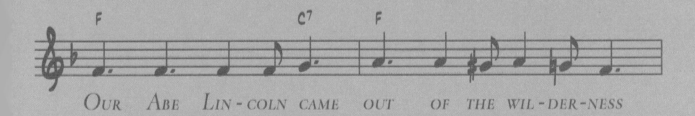

OUR ABE LIN - COLN CAME OUT OF THE WIL - DER - NESS

MAN - Y PROUD YEARS A - GO.